CONTENTS

WHO IS PAUL MCCARTNEY?

Paul McCartney began his musical career writing songs with John Lennon. They are regarded as the most **influential** writing partnership in popular music. Their group, the Beatles, is seen as the most successful of all time. 'Yesterday', Paul's best-known **composition**, is the most recorded song in history. By the end of the 20th Century it had been played on American radio more than seven million times.

A gifted multi-instrumentalist who does not read music, Paul's **melodic** bass guitar playing style has been much copied by other musicians. He has been the only Beatle to remain in the public eye. John Lennon of the Beatles divided his time after the group split up between a **solo** career and being a house-husband, until his murder in 1980. George Harrison and Ringo Starr, the other Beatles, gradually stopped making regular albums, as their solo work became less popular. Paul remains a high profile and hard working rock star – playing to huge crowds and selling millions of records.

A MAN OF MANY TALENTS

Paul is a shrewd businessman. His own successful songs, and the **copyright** he owns on stage shows and the songs of other musicians, have made him one of rock's richest performers.

Despite his wealth, Paul has also tried to lead as ordinary a life as possible. When he was a Beatle, Paul's face was so well known he was mobbed whenever he appeared in public. To avoid the attention of fans he occasionally ventured out disguised with a false moustache and glasses.

Paul is also a devoted family man. Two of his best loved songs, 'Yesterday' and 'Let It Be' were inspired by the death of his mother. His long and happy marriage to Linda McCartney was a love-story of its own. All his children went to **state schools**, and have been carefully guarded from television and newspaper journalists.

Paul returns to a replica of the Cavern Club, Liverpool, to publicize his new album 'Run Devil Run', in December 1999. The last time Paul played the Cavern was with the Beatles in 1963.

EARLY DAYS

P aul was born at Walton Hospital, Liverpool, on 18 June 1942. He was the first child of Jim and Mary McCartney. At the time, Europe was in the middle of the Second World War. Liverpool, then Britain's greatest port, had been bombed so badly that two-thirds of all homes in the city had been damaged or destroyed.

The McCartneys were not wealthy, but Paul's parents had solid jobs and ambitions for themselves and their children. In peacetime, Paul's father Jim worked as a cotton salesman, but his wage was never enough to allow his wife to give up her job as a nurse. In the 1940s and '50s, most women left work when they married, and Jim McCartney was embarrassed by the fact that his wife not only worked, but that she earned more money than he did.

OUTSIDE LAVATORIES

When the war ended in 1945 the family moved to a new **council estate** in Speke, on the outskirts of the city. Built to replace some of the 10,000 homes demolished by German bombs, Speke's barely-finished houses, all with outside lavatories, were surrounded by the dirt and chaos of a huge building site. 'We were slopping through mud for a year,' recalled Paul, looking back on his family's time in this bleak, windswept estate. 'We were always on the edge of the world … there was a feeling you might drop off.'

Being on 'the edge of the world' meant an hour on the bus into Liverpool, but it also meant the McCartneys were right next to the countryside. A five-minute bike ride took Paul to thick woods and fields, and the wide-open skies and mud-flats of the Mersey Estuary. The McCartney family spent many hours bird-spotting and rambling, and the experience left Paul with a life-long love of the countryside and simple pleasures.

Jim McCartney and his famous son in 1964. As a child, Paul was encouraged to play music by his father. The two remained close throughout Jim's life.

GREAT EXPECTATIONS

Speke was a rough estate, with its share of bullies and thugs, but Jim and Mary McCartney were determined that their sons would grow up to be respectable citizens. The boys were discouraged from speaking in the local accent by their mother. The whole family would work together to solve the daily newspaper crossword, and any query Paul or his brother Michael had about the world was resolved by consulting the encyclopaedias Jim had bought to educate his children. When Paul won an essay competition at school he chose a book about modern artists as his prize. It was the start of a life-long interest in paintings and art.

The McCartney parents wanted Paul to be a doctor. When, aged 11, he won a place at the Liverpool Institute, they must have felt he was heading in the right direction. The Institute was the city's best secondary school. It was on his hour-long journey to the Institute that he met George Harrison. George was also studying at the Institute and became one of Paul's best friends. Although Paul was never a brilliant

The house in Allerton where Paul and his family moved in 1955.

GOODGE PLACE

Paul in 1964, at the wheel of another symbol of the 1960s, a Mini. The Beatles would soon be swapping such humble cars for Rolls Royces.

student, the Institute gave Paul the confidence to feel there was a life outside the narrow horizons of working-class Liverpool.

STEPPING UP IN THE WORLD

This feeling of **optimism** was felt throughout Britain. As the country recovered from the Second World War, a generation grew up secure in the knowledge that their world would be different from that of their parents. The British post-war government introduced **social reforms** which ensured that the children of Paul McCartney's generation would be healthier and better educated than ever before.

In 1955 the McCartneys took another step up in the world. The family moved to the middle-class suburb of Allerton. Although they still rented their house from the Liverpool council, for the first time in their lives they had an indoor lavatory. Money was still scarce, though. Looking back on his childhood, Paul said, 'We never had a car. I was the first one in my family to buy a car with my Beatles' earnings.'

FAMILY TRAGEDY

The year 1956 brought family tragedy. In October, when Paul was 14, Mary McCartney died suddenly. A brave, selfless woman, she had ignored the chest pains that had recently troubled her, and developed breast cancer. By the time her condition was discovered, it was too late to save her. 'It was very tough to take,' recalled Paul. 'Seeing your father cry for the first time in your life was not easy.'

The distraught family were lucky to have a close network of relatives who rallied round to help. It was about this time that Paul discovered he had a serious talent for music. His father was musical, and had played piano in a jazz band. Jim had given Paul a trumpet, but this was soon traded in for a guitar. Paul, who is left-handed, discovered that if he restrung the guitar upside-down then he could play quite well. The instrument became a major

Rock and Roll!

Times were changing in late 1950s Britain. The country was thriving, and jobs were easy to come by. For the first time ever, teenagers had money to spend on fashion and entertainment. The music they listened to was **rock and roll** and Paul quickly took to this new music too. He was soon learning the Elvis Presley, Little Richard and Chuck Berry songs he heard on the radio.

A legend in waiting. Paul, porting a rocker quiff and oozing self-confidence, in a Liverpool Institute photograph from the late 1950s.

distraction and comfort, and Paul took it with him everywhere. At the age of 14 he wrote his first song, 'I Lost My Little Girl'. Music gradually became more important than any of his studies, even art, which he liked but did not feel he was very good at.

One summer afternoon, shortly after his 15th birthday, Paul McCartney put on his sharpest clothes and prepared to wander over to a local church **fête**. He was hoping he might meet a girl there. Instead, he met a fellow teenager called John Lennon. Between them, they would change the face of popular music, and become the most successful songwriting partnership of all time.

When Paul arrived at the **fête** he met a band called the Quarrymen. John Lennon was their lead singer. With his aggressive manner, John wasn't immediately easy to get along with, but everything changed when Paul picked up a guitar. He played Eddie Cochran's 'Twenty Flight Rock', a number he fondly describes as 'the song that got me into the Beatles'. The Quarrymen were impressed by his ability to play difficult chords and 'the fiddly bits' in the song. He was in.

Soon after joining, Paul heard his Institute friend George Harrison had started to play guitar. George joined the group in early 1958. The band that was to become the Beatles had virtually fallen into place.

The summer of that year bought another tragedy. John Lennon's mother Julia walked in front of a bus and was killed. Her death affected John very deeply, but the incident brought him and Paul closer together. 'We were both wounded animals and, just looking at each other, we knew the pain we were feeling,' remembered Paul.

The beatles are born

Like most bands, the Quarrymen played songs written by other songwriters. As the Quarrymen got better, John and Paul started writing songs together. Reminiscing to *Guitarist* magazine in early 2000, Paul said, 'We'd turn up to a **gig** and often there'd be four or five bands on. You'd ... discover that the other groups were doing your set. (That's) the reason John and I began writing our own songs. It was the only way of saving our act.'

The original Beatles line-up. Paul is on the piano. John is on the right, and George is second from the right.

After going through various **line-up** and name changes the group called themselves the Beatles. The name is a pun on their style of music, which was known at the time as 'beat music'. Along with Paul, John and George there was bass player Stuart Sutcliffe, and drummer Pete Best.

A LUCKY BREAK

Their first big break was a run of **gigs** in the German port of Hamburg in 1960. It was a harsh introduction to the world of show business. The group lived in appalling **squalor** in filthy rooms behind the screen of a local cinema – they even washed in the cinema toilets. They would play long into the night to drunken sailors. Returning to bed at dawn, their sleep would be interrupted all too soon by booming cinema loudspeakers. During their time in Hamburg, Stuart Sutcliffe left, and Paul switched from guitar to bass. They also adopted their famous 'moptop' haircuts. In those days it was quite daring for men to wear their hair so long. It was an exciting time for Paul – he met artists and students who opened his eyes to a world quite different to the one he'd known in Liverpool.

The Beatles returned to England as hardened professionals, who knew exactly how to entertain a crowd. They played regularly at the Cavern Club in

The Beatles in Hamburg in 1960. From left to right are Pete Best, George Harrison, John Lennon, Paul, and Stuart Sutcliffe.

Liverpool in 1961, and it was here they first became hugely popular. Queues of fans would form around the block whenever they played.

As word of the Beatles live act spread, queues for their Cavern shows began to stretch around the block. The Beatles played the Cavern almost 300 times.

POLISHING UP THEIR ACT

Their popularity attracted the attention of local businessman Brian Epstein. He instinctively knew they could be hugely successful. 'I was immediately struck by their music, their beat, and their sense of humour … and even afterwards when I met them, I was struck again by their personal charm,' he told a TV reporter in 1963.

Epstein became their manager, and the first thing he did was polish up their image. He replaced the dated leather stage clothes they wore with daringly cut suits, and then obtained a **record contract** for his boys. Epstein adored them with the passion of a true fan. The Beatles too were keenly aware of his contribution to their success. 'If anyone was the fifth Beatle it was Brian,' said Paul.

This ridiculous style brings out the worst in boys physically. It makes them look like morons.'
Headmaster John Weightman, on why Beatles' haircuts were banned at his school.

READY TO ROCK ...

The group signed to record company EMI. Here they met a classically-trained Londoner called George Martin, who became their producer. Martin had made a name for himself producing comedy records. He felt an immediate bond with the wisecracking Beatles. But he also recognized how talented they were musically. 'He could see beyond what we were offering him,' said Paul. Martin felt their drummer was weak, so Pete Best was replaced by another Liverpudlian who went by the name of Ringo Starr. The Beatles were set for stardom.

In October 1962 they released their first single, 'Love Me Do'. The song had been written mainly by Paul when he was 16 and John helped him to finish it. It climbed to number 17 in the British pop charts and stirred up enough interest for a follow-up.

... READY TO ROLL

In February 1963 another Lennon-McCartney song, 'Please Please Me', topped the British music charts. This was the beginning of an unbroken run of chart success. The next eleven Lennon-McCartney penned

'The Fabs' in 1962. Pete Best's replacement Ringo Starr is on the left. His brilliant drumming was an essential part of the Beatles' unique sound.

In the plush interior of a London hotel the Beatles and manager Brian Epstein pose for press photographers.

singles would also go to number one in Britain. In March of that year, the first Beatles album, also called 'Please Please Me', topped the album charts.

In the autumn of that year, television appearances caused a sensation in Britain. The newspapers latched on to their popularity, and used the term 'Beatlemania'. By the end of the year the Beatles had become a national **phenomenon**. Meanwhile the Liverpudlian lads had moved down to London – at the time one of the most energetic and exciting cities in the world. Brian Epstein rented a house for them but Paul found himself in the smallest room at the back. Paul hated its lack of homeliness but London became his playground – most nights he went to parties, theatres and clubs.

'Guitars are out'

Before signing to EMI the Beatles auditioned for the Decca record company, but executive Dick Rowe dismissed them: 'Go back to Liverpool, Mr Epstein. Groups with guitars are out.'

17

GLOBAL SUCCESS

Beatlemania was strong enough to cross the Atlantic. In January 1964 the Beatles had their first American number one with the Lennon-McCartney song 'I Wanna Hold Your Hand'. It was time for a visit.

Their arrival at New York's Kennedy Airport in February is still one of those moments that define an era. The Beatles emerged from a Pan Am 707 to a **cacophonous** screaming noise that threatened to drown the howling jet engines of the airport. Five thousand teenagers had arrived to greet them.

As they drove into the city, George Martin recalled; '…every radio station in New York was playing a Beatles record. You could not turn the dial and not find a Beatles record being played.' Martin had had problems interesting the American wing of EMI in the Beatles. 'I got increasingly frustrated because (they would say) "Well, of course. You don't really know about rock 'n'

An ecstatic Paul revels in the adoration of the screaming crowd which turned up to greet the Beatles at New York's Kennedy Airport, in February 1964.

Policemen keep a wary eye on excitable Beatles fans, who have mobbed their hotel in New York, 1964.

roll in England".' The American teenagers' reaction to the Beatles showed how wrong American EMI had been.

CONQUERING HEROES

The impact the Beatles had on the USA was astonishing. The music they played was essentially American. Rock and roll's greatest performers were American. The Beatles' own idols – Elvis Presley, Chuck Berry, Little Richard – were all American. Yet here were four Liverpudlians, barely out of their teens, arriving as conquering heroes.

Their success was down to a magical combination of ingredients. Paul and John had taken their own pop influences and given them a refreshing and original twist. 'They were doing things nobody was doing,' explained Bob Dylan, then one of America's most popular performers. 'Their chords were outrageous, and their harmonies made it all valid. I knew they were pointing to the direction where music had to go.'

Poster advertising the Beatles' second movie, *Help!*

Looking good

Image has always been important to pop success – and the Beatles looked the part. Their daringly tailored suits and, for the time, outrageously long hair, made them unique. They were also funny, and each Beatle had his own personality. George was dark and mysterious; Ringo was **gawky** and cuddly; John was sharp and witty; and Paul was the cute one that girls could imagine taking home to meet their mother.

But there was another, darker reason for their success. Three months before their arrival, American President John F Kennedy had been gunned down in Dallas. A glamorous and much admired figure, Kennedy had symbolized the hopes and dreams of the USA, and the entire nation was deeply shocked by his death. The American media used the arrival of

Beatles on the big screen

In 1964 the Beatles began work on their first movie, *A Hard Day's Night*. The low-budget black and white film was released in July. None of the Beatles had acting experience so the film was filled with action scenes and humorous one-liners. For Paul, who had become interested in drama, it was exciting to work closely with scriptwriters and actors. In 1965 the Beatles made *Help!* It was filmed in the Bahamas in lavish colour. Finally, in 1968 they released *Yellow Submarine*, a feature-length animation.

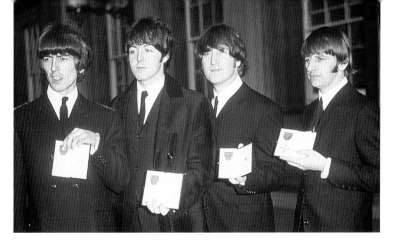

the 'Fab Four' to lighten up people's lives. The Beatles were everywhere, and by April, the top five slots in the American music chart were all Beatles' singles.

FAME AND FORTUNE

The fact that the Beatles could make **rock and roll** music opened American ears to other British groups such as the Rolling Stones. The so-called 'British Invasion', which followed the success of the Beatles, made stars of many British performers. It is thanks to Paul McCartney and John Lennon that the rock and roll industry is seen by the world as an essentially American *and* British **phenomenon**.

The Beatles international success was to make lots of money for the British economy. In recognition of this, each of the Beatles was awarded with a **MBE**. The reported reaction of the two songwriting Beatles showed up their different personalities. John Lennon sneered, 'I thought you had to drive tanks and win wars to get a MBE.' Paul remarked, 'I think it's marvellous.'

SUCCESS AT A PRICE

In August of 1965 the Beatles played Shea Stadium, in New York, to a then-record audience of 56,000. But constant **hysterical** screaming at concerts ruined live performances for the Beatles – it simply wasn't fun any more. Their popularity also attracted death-threats, and the group even began to fear for their lives.

Looking back on that time, Paul remembered, 'As we waited for an armoured car to take us to our guarded hotel rooms, I would say to myself, "I don't want to go through this any longer".' Their **gig** at Candlestick Park in San Francisco, in August 1966, was to be their last ever concert performance.

John, Paul and Ringo survey the sights in New York's Central Park, February 1964. Paul loved the city, but it was John who eventually settled there after the Beatles broke up.

But America had given the Beatles, and Paul, a great deal. Paul fell in love with New York from the moment he arrived. He was thrilled to stand in the places he had seen on television or in Hollywood movies. But Paul was also drawn to New York for more personal reasons. In both America and Europe he was surrounded by people who hero-worshipped him, which made even popping out to the shops for a paper and pint of milk dangerous. New York was massive and Paul found he could walk the streets without being chased by fans. He loved the adoration and wealth that Beatlemania was bringing, but deep inside he also longed to lead a normal life.

Paul in the mid-1960s. The moptop is getting longer, but Paul never grew his hair as long as the other Beatles.

'Yesterday'

Paul wrote one of his most famous songs 'Yesterday' in June 1965. He woke up with the tune running around his head. 'I didn't believe I'd written it. I went around for weeks playing the chords of the song to people, asking them, "Is this like something?"'

Before he wrote the final words, the song was known as 'Scrambled Eggs'. The opening line was, 'Scrambled eggs, oh my baby how I love your legs.'

ROCK GOD

One of the fads of the 1960s was an interest in Indian religion. This led the Beatles to visit India in 1968. Jane Asher is sitting to Paul's right.

For the remainder of the 1960s Paul and John were rock's ruling partnership. Worshipped by both fans and critics, they continued to write songs that brought them wealth and popularity.

During the mid-60s Paul was in a relationship with actress Jane Asher, and lived in her parent's Georgian house in central London. Jane's circle of friends opened Paul's mind to many new influences. As a boy he had loved art and theatre, and being with

Jane exposed him to classical music, and **avant-garde** theatre, art and music. This suited Paul, who was anxious to make up for gaps in his education. He was also constantly searching for fresh ideas. He said at the time, 'As far as the Beatles are concerned … it can get dull if we're not trying to expand and move on to other things.'

Jane and Paul announced their engagement on Christmas day, 1967, but they split up seven months later.

Meeting Linda

In 1967 Paul met American photographer Linda Eastman at a club in London. Linda's father, Lee, was a top show-business lawyer, and she grew up in a house full of music. Lee was also a great art lover and was wealthy enough to collect the work of famous painters. Linda combined her childhood influences of art and music in a career as a rock photographer. It was through contacts here that she met Paul. They found they had a mutual interest in art, and a shared affection for the music of their parent's generation.

Paul's instant new family, photographer Linda Eastman and her daughter Heather. Ringo Starr is on the right.

Like Paul, Linda had also lost her mother at an early age – she died in a plane crash when Linda was just 18. At their first meeting Paul was still with Jane Asher and Linda had her own life in New York with her daughter Heather. But in 1968 Paul called Linda up again. Linda got on a plane to London. They fell in love and married in March 1969. Their first child, Mary, was born in August of that year.

THE SWINGING SIXTIES

Although they had stopped touring, the Beatles were busier than ever. In May 1967 they released 'Sgt Pepper's Lonely Hearts Club Band' – an album many regard as the musical high-point of the 1960s. Among their other triumphs were the double album 'The Beatles' and the film, *Yellow Submarine*.

Artist Peter Blake's legendary cover for the 'Sgt Pepper' album. Surrounding the Beatles are photographs of their heroes.

THE BEGINNING OF THE END

Beatles producer George Martin remarked on the **rivalry** that lay at the heart of McCartney and Lennon's songwriting partnership. 'John sneered at a lot of things, but that was part of the **collaboration** between them. If John did something, Paul would wish he'd thought of it and go away and try and do

'Never had it so good ...'

The late-1960s was an extraordinary time to be young. Jobs were even easier to come by than in the 1950s, and many social attitudes, for example to class, were changing. Young people really believed they could change the world. They believed that rock music, with Paul and John at the helm, would help to bring about that change.

something better and vice versa.' But Paul and John would also co-operate. Journalist Hunter Davies, who spent time with the group in 1967 and '68 wrote: 'They'd each give the other bits of songs they'd written. Now and again they'd have written whole songs but mostly it was half a song, and the other would help finish it.'

But all was not well. In August 1967, at the height of their popularity, manager Brian Epstein died of an overdose of sleeping pills. He suffered from depression, and no one knows for sure whether his death was accidental or suicide. Looking back on this time, John recalled, 'After Brian died we collapsed. Paul took over and supposedly led us. But … we went round in circles.'

The Beatles began to squabble. John and Paul worked more on their own material, rather than as songwriting partners, and Paul and George's relationship began to break down.

DIFFICULT TIMES

In February 1968 the Beatles set up their own company, Apple. At the time, Paul explained how he intended it to run. 'We want to help people ... we're in a happy position of not needing any more money, so for the first time the bosses aren't in it for profit. If you come to me and say, "I've had such-and-such a dream," I'll say to you, "Go away and do it".'

The Apple Boutique, one arm of the Beatles' business venture, gives away clothes on the day it stops trading in 1968.

Run by friends, the company was a financial disaster. Staff spent money like water, and the office was flooded with unworkable business ideas. The Beatles were losing around £20,000 a week and the group looked for a business manager to rescue them. John, George and Ringo favoured a tough American businessman named Allen Klein, but Paul was keen to use his father-in-law, Lee Eastman. This difference between them would never be resolved and would lead to an ugly end to the Beatles' extraordinary story.

During this time John had also begun a relationship with Japanese artist, Yoko Ono. She remained constantly by his side during recording sessions, which irritated Paul and the other Beatles considerably.

'The Long and Winding Road'

Work on their album 'Let It Be' was filmed. It proved to be a depressing record of the end of the relationship between each of the Beatles. Despite this, the album contains two of Paul's best Beatles **ballads** – 'The Long and Winding Road', and 'Let It Be'. Both songs were a reflection of the hurt he felt at the slow break-up of the group.

The Beatles' career ended with 'Abbey Road' which is now regarded as one of their finest albums. Listening to this last great outpouring of Beatle creativity is exhilarating and sad, and it stands as a great **memorial** to the most creative and influential group of the 20th Century.

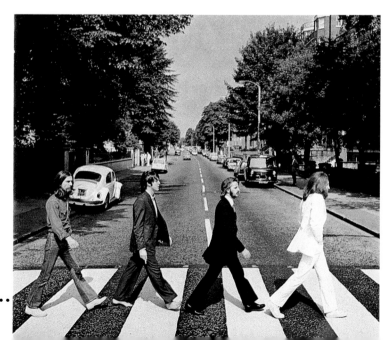

The Beatles walk over a zebra crossing outside their recording studio in London. The shot was used on the cover of their final album 'Abbey Road'.

OUT OF FAVOUR

Although John had told the other Beatles he wanted to leave the group, it was Paul who eventually made their split public. He announced in April 1970 that the Beatles would never work together again.

At the end of the year, on the advice of his father-in-law Lee Eastman, he sued the other Beatles to end their business partnership. It was a terribly painful time for Paul, but he was determined to rescue his finances from the clutches of Allen Klein, whom he was convinced was acting dishonestly.

'I had to take the other Beatles to court. And I got a lot of guilt off that,' Paul recalled. That wasn't all he got. When the case came to court Paul won, and the Beatles' financial partnership was dissolved. After the verdict, the other Beatles drove round to Paul's London house, and John put a couple of bricks through his windows.

'I didn't leave the Beatles – the Beatles have left the Beatles, but no one wants to be the one to say the party's over.'
Paul McCartney, 1970.

'THE PARTY'S OVER'

Looking back on the months following the Beatles' split, Paul said, 'I found myself in the morning not wanting to get up….When I did get up I went straight to the whisky. Luckily, Linda was there. She kept me straight.'

As he had done in other difficult times of his life, Paul lost himself in his music. In 1970 he released his first **solo** album 'Paul McCartney'. The cover had a photograph of a bearded Paul cuddling his baby Mary, and contained a catchy single 'Maybe I'm Amazed' – considered by many to be his most successful solo song. The album 'Ram' followed shortly after.

Divided by squabbles over money the Beatles were increasingly uncomfortable with each other, as this photograph from the late 1960s shows.

Flying solo

Paul also put a group together with Linda and a selection of other musicians, called Wings. Although his recordings, either as a **solo** artist or with Wings sold well, Paul was out of favour with the critics. They complained that his solo work was shallow. Paul was also seen as 'the Beatle who broke up the Beatles' – given their popularity, this was not a happy position in which to be.

Out on his own. Paul in the early 1970s.

Bitter rivalry

Paul's albums also seemed particularly uninspired when compared with the solo work of his ex-partner, and rival, John Lennon. At the time he was hitting new creative peaks with 'John Lennon/Plastic

Paul and John

Paul spoke movingly about his falling out with John Lennon, in Barry Miles's biography *Many Years From Now*. 'When John did "How Do You Sleep?" I didn't want to get into a slanging match. I just let him do it, because he was being fed a lot of those lines by Klein and Yoko....Part of it was cowardice: John was a great wit, and I didn't want to go fencing with the rapier champion.... I always find myself wanting to excuse John's behaviour, just because I loved him.'

Ono Band' and 'Imagine'. John was even attacking Paul in song, in 'How Do You Sleep?' John used Liverpudlian street talk to sneer, 'Those freaks was right when they said you was dead,' and, 'The only thing you done was yesterday.'

Paul and John went through several bad years in the early 1970s, but Paul was always keen to patch things up with his old friend, who had now moved to the USA. 'I would ring him when I went to New York and he would say, "Yeah, what d'you want?"… It was all very **acrimonious** and bitter,' he recalled.

John Lennon works on a song with partner Yoko Ono. Yoko increasingly replaced Paul as John's creative partner.

Family and friends

The rift between Paul and John was healed by an extraordinary show of good will by the McCartneys. In 1973, John and Yoko split up, and John went to live in Los Angeles. During their separation Yoko visited Paul and Linda in London. Despite their differences, the McCartneys were friendly and sympathetic to Yoko, and even agreed to speak to John about getting back together with her. They visited Los Angeles, met with John and helped to bring John and Yoko back together.

After that John and Paul were friends again, and when the McCartneys went to New York they would often visit the Lennons. Paul and Linda had a young family at the time, and John and Yoko had just had a son, Sean. The two ex-Beatles would often talk about children.

'People say **domesticity** is the enemy of art … but I made my decision and I feel okay with it. **Ballads** and babies – that's what happened to me.'
Paul McCartney, quoted in *Rock – The Rough Guide.*

At home

At the time the McCartneys had three daughters – Heather, from Linda's previous marriage, Mary, and Stella, who had been born in 1971. The McCartney family would be completed by son James, born in 1977. Paul's love of children is well-known: 'I'd been fortunate to be around a lot of kids. I'm from a big family so your cousins would dump a baby on you and you'd know how to jiggle it and you became good at it … I've enjoyed being a parent, just never had a problem with it….'

Paul and his family in 1973. Heather hugs her mum, who also carries baby Stella. Daughter Mary stands in front of Paul.

'BAND ON THE RUN'

In 1973 Paul McCartney and Wings packed their bags and headed for Lagos, Nigeria, to record a new album. The trip started badly – Paul and Linda were held at gunpoint by armed robbers, and Linda pleaded, 'Please don't shoot him! He's a Beatle!'

The new album was called 'Band on the Run'. It was a critical and commercial triumph and considered by many people to be the best ever work by a former Beatle. Two singles from the album, 'Band on the Run' and 'Jet', were huge successes.

Sporting what passed for high fashion in 1973, Paul's group Wings mime one of their singles in a television studio.

Things also began to look up as Paul's relationship with the other ex-Beatles got better. They had realized that Paul had been right to be suspicious of Allen Klein and no longer wanted him to manage their finances either.

RECORD SALES

In 1975 Wings released their follow-up to 'Band on the Run'. It was called 'Venus and Mars', but it was a serious critical and commercial disappointment. Then, in 1978 Paul released the love-it-or-loathe-it

'Mull of Kintyre'. It sold two million copies in the UK, and at the time was the biggest selling single ever released in the UK. Other singles, such as 'Silly Love Songs' and 'Let 'Em In', were also extremely successful. Paul could still create best-selling records.

'Mull of Kintyre'

Paul has several homes. He bought a farm near the Mull of Kintyre in Scotland, during his Beatles' days. Its secluded location was a welcome retreat from the spotlight of London, and the madness of Beatlemania. 'I liked its isolation and I liked the privacy and the end-of-the-world remoteness compared to a city,' he explained. Linda loved it, and Scotland, too. 'It was the most beautiful land you have ever seen … so different from all the hotels and limousines and the music business.…' she said.

Paul and Linda go boating. The former Beatle and his wife in the mid-1970s enjoy a quiet moment together.

DOWNS AND UPS

In December 1980 John Lennon was shot dead in New York by a **deranged** fan. Journalists immediately gathered around Paul's house. He commented, 'I can't take it in at the moment. John was a great man who'll be remembered for his unique contributions to art, music and world peace.' Then, as he always had done at terrible times in his life, he buried himself in work, travelling to a London studio to spend the day recording.

Later that day, Paul was again harassed by journalists eager for a quote. With microphones pushed in his face, a tired and upset Paul reacted to the journalist's question, 'How do you feel about John's murder?' with the response, 'It's a drag!'

This offhand and seemingly uncaring remark was seized upon by unfriendly television and newspaper journalists, and widely reported. Paul later explained, 'What I meant was ... "Don't invade my privacy"... When I got home I wept buckets, in the privacy of my own home.'

Paul was deeply upset by the death of his childhood friend, but he did have the consolation of knowing that he and John had patched up their differences. 'I was able to think, at least we parted on good terms. Thank God for that.' But cruel remarks in music journals about John's killer shooting the wrong Beatle must have stung.

GLOBAL SUPERSTAR

Wings split up in 1980, but Paul continued to push his musical career as a solo performer. In the early 1980s he recorded **duets** with two other giants of pop – Stevie Wonder and Michael Jackson. The results ('Ebony and Ivory', 'The Girl is Mine', respectively) may not have been to everyone's taste, but they were huge commercial successes.

The American ger/songwriter, Stevie Wonder, ith whom Paul ecorded 'Ebony Ivory' in 1982.

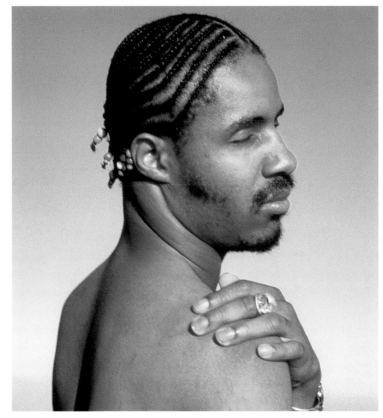

The song is mine

Whilst working with Paul, Michael Jackson had asked Paul for business advice. Paul told him to invest his **royalties** in buying **copyright** on songs. During the conversation, Michael quipped that he would buy Paul's songs. It turned out that he wasn't joking.

In 1985 the copyright holders of Lennon and McCartney's Beatles' songs put them up for auction. Paul had long wanted to own the copyright on his own material and immediately set about trying to buy his songs. But Michael Jackson made a higher bid against him. This missed opportunity was one of the great disappointments of his life. Jackson still owns these songs, and the two men have not spoken since. Paul learned by this experience and has purchased the songs of many other performers and writers.

Lights, camera, action!

In the mid-1980s, Paul made another film. He had been fascinated by the process of film making, ever since the Beatles made their own films in the 1960s. But his production, *Give My Regards To Broad Street* was not a success – the critics hated it and the public stayed away.

A still from *Give My Regards To Broad Street*. Paul hams it up with old pal and Beatles' drummer Ringo Starr.

Music collecting

Paul's father-in-law Lee Eastman has been a major influence on his business activities. Paul has invested much of his money in music, and with Lee's help set about acquiring the copyright to an extraordinary collection of music publishing. Among others, the songs of Buddy Holly and Hoagy Carmichael, and shows such as *A Chorus Line, Annie, Grease,* and *Guys and Dolls,* are now owned by Paul McCartney.

But the failure of the film did nothing to dent Paul's position as one of the world's major performers. In 1985 a huge charity concert called Live Aid was staged at London's Wembley Stadium, and broadcast to a global audience of one and a half billion people. Paul was the performer who closed the show, with a solo piano rendition of 'Let It Be'.

Paul and a host celebrities sing *ed The World'* t the climax of ndon's Live Aid show in 1985.

ON TOUR AGAIN

The 1980s ended on another high. In late 1989 Paul took a new band on a world tour. They visited thirteen countries and played to over 3 million fans. One of the highlights of the tour was a record-breaking crowd of 184,000 who came to see the band perform at the Maracana Stadium in Rio de Janeiro, Brazil.

AN ARTISTIC SIDE

Paul also has a creative life outside music. Encouraged by Linda, and his friend, artist Willem de Kooning, Paul is a keen oil painter. He has completed many portraits and landscapes. Paul has always had an eye for painting and design, and collects works of art. He painted well at school, and helped to design wrapping paper, **publicity** material, and record sleeves during his time with the Beatles. He has always felt unsure of this talent. 'I felt that only people who had gone to art school were allowed to paint,' he told

Charity work

Paul has supported the Nordoff Robbins Music Therapy charity, which uses music to reach severely autistic children. Paul played a concert for the charity, which was televised.

biographer Barry Miles. 'Then I suddenly thought, this is absolute madness. I'm sure a lot of the great painters didn't go to art college.'

He said recently 'I've been painting a lot for the last ten years. I identify very closely with the caveman who painted on the walls. I'm sure he didn't go to art school, but he had a passion, and he did it.'

Paul on stage in the early 1990s. Paul's live shows have broken attendance records around the globe.

Paul Today

In 1991 the world saw yet another side of Paul McCartney's musical talent. In that year he made his classical music debut with a piece called 'The Liverpool Oratorio', which was written together with American composer Carl Davis.

Based on incidents from Paul's own life, the work was performed by the ninety-piece Royal Liverpool Philharmonic Orchestra, four soloists, and a choir. It was warmly received by critics and the public, and has since been performed all over the world.

Paul's affection for his home city remains strong. 'I love Liverpool,' he said recently, 'Every street's got a little memory.' He also credits his connection to the city with his desire for him and his family to lead a normal life: 'The Liverpool connection's great for that.'

Linda too, had a yearning for normality: 'She wanted to keep our feet on the ground – for the kids and us both.... We put them through **state schools** instead of Eton and all the posh schools,' said Paul.

The beatles are back!

In 1995 the Beatles' industry (still in excellent shape with all Beatles' albums re-released on CD and still selling consistently) went into overdrive with the release of three **Anthology** CDs of **demos, out-takes** and alternative versions. Long available as **bootlegs,** they were a fascinating insight into the Beatles' creative process. The CDs sold so well that the Beatles were one of the top three best-selling artists of 1995.

Paul and his touring band return to his roots in June 1990. Behind them is the River Mersey, Liverpool.

While putting the 'Anthology' material together Paul worked again with the two other surviving Beatles, George and Ringo. They jokingly called themselves the 'Threetles', and used a John Lennon demo tape to create two new singles, 'Free As a Bird' and 'Real Love', which were released under the name of the Beatles.

Patron of the arts

Much of Paul's time in the early to mid-1990s was taken up helping to set up the Liverpool Institute of Performing Arts. The idea for the Institute was inspired by the film *Fame*, which portrayed the lives and ambitions of pupils at New York's famous School for the Performing Arts. Paul was asked to be the project's chief **patron,** which gave the project both **credibility** and publicity. After six years the money was finally raised to build the Institute. Paul was delighted that the building chosen to house the project was his old school – the now closed and derelict Liverpool Institute.

Paul returns to Buckingham Palace for a knighthood in 1997. He was delighted with the award.

The new Liverpool Institute was opened by the Queen in 1996. Today, it offers nearly 200 students courses on working in the entertainment industry.

Sir Paul

Paul's contribution to popular music was recognized by a knighthood in 1996. Paul went to the ceremony at Buckingham Palace with his children Mary, Stella and James in March 1997. On that day he told journalists, 'This is one of the best days of my life. To come from a terraced house in Liverpool to this house is quite a journey and I am immensely proud...' He later reflected, 'the nice thing about it, (is) when me and Linda are sitting on holiday, watching the sunset. I turn to her and say, "Hey, you're a Lady"... although she always was anyway.'

The 1990s also saw Linda in the public eye. Her own book of vegetarian recipes, *Linda McCartney's Home Cooking*, sold well. She also created her own highly successful line of meat-free convenience frozen foods.

Paul and Linda had long been two of the country's most famous vegetarians. Their compassion for animals is well known. They once bought land on Exmoor, Devon, to stop stag hunting there. Linda took an especially hard-line on the meat trade. 'We are doing to animals what Hitler did to humans,' she said.

A TERRIBLE BLOW

But the decade was to bring yet another tragedy in Paul's life. In 1998 Linda died. She had been suffering from breast cancer for a couple of years.

'I expected us to be 80-year-olds on the porch on our rocking chairs….' said Paul, speaking on British television in late 1999. Referring to her illness, he went on, 'We fought against it, and did everything we could possibly do. We thought we might have cracked it … so when she died it was just a terrible blow for me and the kids.'

After a year's grieving Paul returned to the public eye. He released a critically acclaimed album called 'Run Devil Run' and appeared on British television. Although he had visibly aged, he talked clear-eyed and fondly of his dead wife, and played two rock and roll songs.

Paul and Linda attend a fashion show in Paris, October 1997. On display are daughter Stella's highly successful ready-to-wear designs. Linda died the following year.

BACK TO HIS ROOTS

As the century ended Paul returned to his roots in Liverpool to play a **gig** at the 'Cavern'. The original Cavern had been knocked down in the 1960s, and this venue was a **reconstruction** of the club in Liverpool's Beatles Museum.

Paul in 1999. He stands in front of a replica of the Cavern stage where the Beatles first played nearly 40 years before.

Paul's fans were delighted and his performance sparked television and newspaper interest throughout the world.

Speaking of his superstar status Paul said, 'I've always had this thing of him and me; he goes on stage, he's famous, and then me; I'm just some kid from Liverpool ... occasionally I stop and think, I am Paul McCartney ... I think it helps keep you sane, actually, if your famous side is a little bit removed from you yourself.'

Paul's music has brought pleasure to millions. To older people, Paul will forever remind them of their youth, in the more carefree days of the 1960s. To up-and-coming musicians and teenage music fans today, Paul's songs are an inspiration. To himself, he may still just be 'some kid from Liverpool', but he is undoubtedly one of the greatest musicians of the 20th Century.

Changing Views of Paul McCartney

A collection of quotes for, by and about Paul McCartney

After absorbing every influence from Fred Astaire and Gene Kelly to Little Richard and Elvis Presley, he came forward as Paul McCartney... neither a rocker nor a balladeer, but an extraordinary hybrid from whom sprang 'Yesterday' and 'Lady Madonna'.

Ray Coleman *McCartney – Yesterday and Today*

He's an artist, and artists are moody.... How much pressure has he had, and how many lives has he lived? So he might come on like he's normal, but there's a lot of pressure in there.

Linda McCartney

People tend to dismiss me as the married ex-Beatle who loves sheep and wrote 'Yesterday'... They think I can write only slushy love songs. My image is more goody-goody than I actually am.

Paul McCartney, *USA Today*, 1989

> That was a songwriting partnership. We were very special. I could feel it was a special kind of thing because it was dead easy to write.... John and I were perfect, really, for each other. I could do stuff he might not be in the mood for; egg him in a certain direction... he could do the same with me.
> Paul McCartney, *The Lost Beatles Interviews* by Geoffrey and Brenda Guillano

Paul McCartney in the 1990s. The aging ex-Beatle still shows no sign of slowing down.

LIST OF FILMS AND RECORDS – SINGLES AND ALBUMS

WITH THE BEATLES

1962
'Love Me Do'

1963
'Please Please Me'
'From Me To You'
'She Loves You'
'I Want To Hold Your Hand'
'Please Please Me' (album)
'With The Beatles' (album)

1964
'Can't Buy Me Love'
'A Hard Day's Night'
'I Feel Fine'
'A Hard Day's Night' (album)
'Beatles For Sale' (album)

1965
'Ticket To Ride'
'Help!'
'Yesterday'
'We Can Work It Out'
'Help!' (album)
'Rubber Soul' (album)

1966
'Paperback Writer'
'Eleanor Rigby'/'Yellow Submarine'
'Revolver' (album)

1967
'Strawberry Fields Forever'/'Penny Lane'
'All You Need Is Love'
'Hello Goodbye'
'Sgt Pepper's Lonely Hearts Club Band'
(album)

1968
'Lady Madonna'
'Hey Jude'
'The Beatles' (album)

1969
'Get Back'
'The Ballad Of John And Yoko'
'Let It Be'
'Yellow Submarine' (album)
'Abbey Road' (album)

1970
'The Long And Winding Road'
'Let It Be' (album)

1994
'The Beatles – Live At The BBC'
(album)

1995
'Free As A Bird'
'Real Love'
'The Beatles Anthology 1' (album)

1996
'The Beatles Anthology 2' (album)
'The Beatles Anthology 3' (album)

WITH WINGS AND AS A SOLO ARTIST

1970
'Maybe I'm Amazed'
'McCartney' (album)

1971
'Uncle Albert'/'Admiral Halsey'
'Ram' (album)

1972
'Give Ireland Back To The Irish'
'Wild Life' (album)

1973
'Hi Hi Hi'/'C Moon'
'Mary Had A Little Lamb'
'My Love'
'Live And Let Die'
'Band On The Run' (album)

1974
'Jet'
'Band On The Run'

1975
'Listen To What The Man Said'
'Venus and Mars' (album)

1976
'Silly Love Songs'
'Let 'Em In'
'Wings At The Speed Of Sound' (album)

1977
'Mull of Kintyre'

1980
'Coming Up'
'McCartney II' (album)

1982
'Tug Of War'
'Ebony and Ivory' (with Stevie Wonder)

1983
'Pipes Of Peace'
'The Girl Is Mine' (with Michael Jackson)
'Say Say Say' (with Michael Jackson)

1984
'No More Lonely Nights'
'Give My Regards to Broad Street' (album)

1986
'Press To Play' (album)

1989
'Flowers In The Dirt' (album)

1991
'Liverpool Oratorio' (album)

1993
'Paul Is Live' (album)

1997
'Flaming Pie' (album)
'Standing Stone' (album)

1999
'Run Devil Run' (album)
'Working Classical' (album)

FILMS

WITH THE BEATLES
1964
A Hard Day's Night

1965
Help!

1967
Magical Mystery Tour

1968
Yellow Submarine

1970
Let It Be

SOLO
1981
Paul McCartney and Wings – Rockshow

1984
Give My Regards To Broad Street

1991
Paul McCartney – The Liverpool Oratorio

1997
Paul McCartney – Standing Stone

The 1994 film *Backbeat* is a creditable dramatization of the Beatles' pre-fame years in Liverpool and Hamburg.

GLOSSARY

acrimonious causing bad feeling

anthology a collection of an artist's work

avant-garde art which is considered to be daring and experimental

ballad a slow, gentle song

bootleg an illicit copy of a recording, sold illegally, for which the artist gets no income

cacophonous loud and disturbing sound

collaboration a partnership on a project between two or more people

composition a musical work

copyright the legal ownership of a song or written work

council estate housing provided by local government

credibility respect and trust in the honesty of an artist's work

demo a rough preliminary recording not intended to be sold to the public

deranged mentally unstable

domesticity home life

duets songs sung by two people

fête an outdoor gala, usually held to raise money for charity

gawky clumsy and awkward

gig a musical performance

hysterical in a frenzied emotional state, especially including uncontrollable crying, screaming or laughing

influential making people want to copy what you are doing

line-up the personnel in a group

MBE (Member of the British Empire) a medal given by the British government in recognition of a person's achievements.

melodic a musical term meaning pleasantly tuneful

memorial something that commemorates a person who has died

optimism a state of mind where one expects things to improve or turn out for the best

out-take a recording which is not released to the public

patron a powerful person who supports a particular individual or cause

phenomenon an unusual and remarkable occurrence

publicity information used to stir up interest in a person or a group, which appears in the press, broadcasting and other media

quiff a type of haircut where the hair is combed into a tuft above the forehead. This style was popular with British teddy boys – a delinquent youth cult in 1950s Britain.

reconstruction something that has been built to resemble something else

record contract an agreement between a group or individual and a record company where the company sells recordings produced by that group or individual

rivalry competition between people, often aggressive or driven by ill-feeling

rock and roll a type of guitar and drum based music, which blends rhythm and blues and country and western styles

royalties payment made to artists whenever their work is sold or performed

social reform government-backed policies intended to make life better for poorer people

solo performing as an individual artist, rather than as part of a group

squalor dirty and repulsive conditions

state schools government funded schools, which pupils attend for free

INDEX